Journeying
Through the Days 2011

A Calendar and Journal for Personal Reflection

UPPER
ROOM BOOKS®
NASHVILLE

> *For more ideas about deepening your Christian spiritual practice, visit The Upper Room Web site: www.upperroom.org*

Chasing Words, Chasing Light

R. Grace Imathiu

As I sat down to write this introduction, I received an e-mail from David Hay Jones, the photographer for this year's *Journeying Through the Days*. He was writing from a town in Sweden, sixty kilometers north of the Arctic Circle, where he was taking some of the pictures that will cheer you on as you journal this year. Unlike the journaler who is armed with pen and paper and chases words to nail a thought, feeling, or hunch, David journals with his camera. Although at first glance his subject seems to be the beautiful wild places in our world, his primary subject is light. "I chase the light," he once remarked.

David wrote: "What a journey *Journeying* has been. I am just wrapping up a year's photography. I've spent a week trekking across a huge area of wetland and mountains in Lapland. I've seen moose, bear, lynx, and reindeer. Only this morning I saw a peregrine falcon circling overhead, screeching. I've been stung by mosquitoes and bitten by every imaginable kind of crawling insect. It's been a fantastic year!"

Throughout his year of taking the photographs that grace this journal, David e-mailed me snippets of his adventures in remote regions. The details often exhausted me even before I looked at the photographs. I am not one to spend days in my own company, slogging through marshes and climbing mountains as my skin becomes covered with insect bites and stings. I prefer to engage the beautiful great outdoors with clean boots from a convenient viewpoint. Perhaps it is because of my busy life, so crammed with demands, that I rarely find the time to venture from the well-beaten path into new territory.

David's deep passion and respect for wild places is contagious. He encourages us to try moving away from the familiar to explore other possibilities. I have learned to stop my inherent multitasking—to pause and observe the patterns hidden in the details of a leaf or an insect's wing, to arise early and watch the morning light transform an everyday landscape into magic. David urges us to watch and see "what the light is doing." With practice I have learned to see how the light turns ripe coffee beans almost into drops of blood on the slopes of Mount Kenya. I have watched the light turn snow into diamonds in Wisconsin's winter wonderland. Time and time again, I have been awed by how the gentle evening light can transform even the dullest scenes into a breathtaking mystery.

THE JOURNALER AS EXPLORER AND ARTIST

Just as a photographer travels to remote regions and wild places, so the journaler travels and explores what philosopher Lévi-Strauss called "the national parks of the mind."[1] We often neglect the "national parks" of our inner life in our busy lives, and we leave untapped their gifts and healing power. Like the photographer, the journaler is encouraged to dare trek through the inner terrain and, armed with pen and paper, try to capture an experience, a beauty, or an emotion with words and at times with silence.

Like the photographer, the journaler is an explorer and artist. Words are the tools the journaler employs, sometimes filling page after page with ink, and other times allowing the empty space to offer times of rest and another kind of listening.

A VARIETY OF JOURNALING STYLES

The journaler paces herself without the guilt of obligation and duty. One journal entry may be a coherent reflection that reads like a well-thought-out article, while another entry reads like a psalm, a lament, or a prayer tossed to God for God to complete. Yet another page may describe physical surroundings, while another contains a grocery list of words or the same word or name over and over like a mantra. Sometimes the handwriting may be neat and careful, as though penned in the quiet of a library; at other times it may be legible only to the writer, who seems to have written while riding on a camel's back! Perhaps the writing itself, the act of putting pen to paper, is very much part and parcel of journaling. It engages another way of being that is not engaged when we sit at a computer and tap away at the keyboard.

There is no "correct" way of journaling. Some people journal in prose, others in poetry, and others allow a stream of unconsciousness to bleed itself out. Some journal about what is going on around them, others journal about their dreams, and others journal as a way to unlock secrets from their past or make decisions for their future. You need not adopt or learn a correct journaling voice. Unlike the photographer of this journal, whose audience is diverse, the journal writer pens words for only one audience: the self.

THE GIFTS OF JOURNALING

Journaling offers the gift of writing without the baggage of expectations from an audience waiting to be entertained, enlightened, or enriched. An audience, whether imagined or real, often influences our voice, vocabulary, and content as we enter the game of writing for effect—giving people what we think they need, rather than being blunt about what we want to discover, unearth, or examine closely. When writing for an audience, we try to craft a coherent presentation, which requires a posture of expertise.

In contrast, journal writing invites us into a no-holds-barred, frank conversation with ourselves. Such a conversation not only allows openness but also demands an honesty we might not find with anyone else. The space this creates allows us to speak accurately about our condition.

At times I have found it helpful to accurately identify emotions such as anger, fear, and even animosity. My grandmother used to say, "Half the medicine is calling the illness by its name." However, in my vocation as a pastor, I am not comfortable, nor would many around me feel comfortable, if I admitted having these strong and often dreaded emotions. I therefore more often speak of my anger as disappointment, my fear as concern, and my animosity as discomfort.

In seeking my grandmother's "half the medicine," journaling often has provided me with space for honesty in naming. Poet Gary Snyder wrote, "If you speak to the condition of your times with some accuracy and intention, then it may speak to the future, too."[2]

Journaling is self-care. So many of us are so busy that we neglect to nurture our core, our souls. We forget to ask and explore questions such as:

- Am I content?
- How do I build deep contentment?
- What do I want to do with my life?
- How can I build a sense of growth and spiritual development that takes me beyond the mundane?

Although we may get away with ignoring these questions for a while, the questions do not go away but find places in our lives to nest and hatch into general dissatisfactions about pretty much everything. The discipline of regular journaling gives these questions an excellent place to come out in the open and at least be recognized, if not tackled. In turn, the exercise unclutters our minds and spirits so we can pursue the light.

Over time, we gain confidence and become accustomed to giving ourselves time each day to express our thoughts, delve a little deeper. The deeper we travel into our inner life, looking more closely at what we want from life, what we can give, what we would like to share, and what we need and need to do, the more fulfilled our outer life becomes. Journaling is self-care for the sake of ourselves and those who love us. Through journaling, we learn to understand ourselves better so we can let go of events, memories, and behavior that cause us anxiety.

Getting Started

You may wonder, *How do I begin such a valuable inner journey?* There are no arcane secrets. Those who journal on a regular basis will point to a baby who learns to walk with baby steps, a runner who begins her training with slow runs and then builds up, or a pianist who begins by practicing and repeating simple tunes. Journaling begins with a few words, perhaps not your most profound words but your words nevertheless, marks on a piece of paper. The simplest form is diary notes—recording what you have done during the day or what remains to be done. This is nothing more than a captain's log of daily life. It is amazing how simple sentences from what seems to be a mundane life, when read in light of the passage of time, become almost magical and evoke so many memories.

My journaling has afforded me many opportunities to record blissful moments of grace: my baby's first steps and his first words; my son's first school report; an achievement of a personal goal; the repayment of a loan. Last autumn I recorded an incident after going for many weeks without any journaling. I was reflecting on how I am constantly surprised and shaken at the creative way my eight-year-old son sees the world in ways that escape my eyes. That day while we were walking on a favorite trail, I was noticing how fall leaves in the shifting light suddenly glow as the dipping sun washes over them. Erik, on the other hand, was totally fascinated by the movements of an insect upon a twig, attempting to figure out how it managed to get its six legs working in unison. He asked, "Momma, have you ever wondered what it's like to be a bug?" That thought struck me as I replied, "No, I've never wondered what it is like to be a bug." Thank you, Erik, for that new insight!

Likewise, David's eye for detail has helped me look at the world in a fresh and different way. Through his photography I have learned that a chipmunk is indeed a handsome little creature when you look at its face up close. I have come to see the remarkable similarity between a dragonfly and the first aircraft; I have observed how pomegranates contain hundreds of what look like ruby tears. I now understand that a trek taking you over dozens of bug-bitten miles is worth the toil when you can stand atop a peak and look out over lakes and rivers glistening like jewels in the evening light.

As you begin your journaling year, may these photographs keep you company, inspire and engage you, and shed light on the terrain of your inner life. As you journal as both explorer and artist, may you find the sense of awe, curiosity, fascination, and willingness to be surprised that the photographer has found.

Whether you journal every day or allow yourself many blank pages, may your journaling invite you to dig deeper and tackle life's tough questions. When you cannot find the right word to express your thought or experience, may you playfully use the tools you have in a novel combination.

But best of all, as you journal, may you be willing to accept and tolerate the occasional sting of a tear and the spiritual mud on your boots and hands. The healing gifts of the inner life that await you are well worth the work. Happy journaling!

The Reverend Grace Imathiu is a Methodist minister who has served congregations in Kenya, Washington, Ohio, Tennessee, and Wisconsin. An ordained elder in the Methodist Church in Kenya, she is in demand around the world as a preacher and Bible study teacher. Grace is the author of Words of Fire, Spirit of Grace.

1. Claude Lévi-Strauss, quoted in Gary Snyder, The Real Work: Interviews and Talks 1964–1979 (New York: New Directions Publishing, 1980), 132.
2. Snyder, The Real Work ,163.

After they [the Magi] had heard the king, they went on their way, and the star they had seen in the east went ahead of them until it stopped over the place where the child was.

Matthew 2:9, NIV

NEW YEAR'S DAY

[The one who sits on the throne] said, "It is done! I am the Alpha and the Omega, the beginning and the end."

Revelation 21:6, NRSV

Christ's light which comes to us
cannot be kept—hoarded, hid, suppressed.
Christ's light which comes to us
must beam through our lives,
shine on our paths,
and go from us, to be made more in the sharing.

ROBERTA PORTER

EPIPHANY SUNDAY

Paul wrote, "Here I am, preaching and writing about things that are way over my head, the inexhaustible riches and generosity of Christ."

Ephesians 3:8, THE MESSAGE

ISAIAH 60:1-6 · PSALM 72:1-7, 10-14 ·
EPHESIANS 3:1-12 · MATTHEW 2:1-12

The LORD God says to his servant,
"I, the LORD, have called you and
given you power to see that justice is
done on earth."

Isaiah 42:5-6, GNT

Those who fear [God] and do what is
right are acceptable to him, no matter
what race they belong to.

Acts 10:35, GNT

All the prophets spoke about [Jesus],
saying that all who believe in him will
have their sins forgiven through the
power of his name.

Acts 10:43, GNT

EPIPHANY OF THE LORD

The LORD gives strength to his people
and blesses them with peace.

Psalm 29:11, GNT

Jesus came from Galilee to John at the Jordan, to be baptized by him.

Matthew 3:13, NRSV

The voice of the LORD is heard on the seas; the glorious God thunders, and his voice echoes over the ocean.

Psalm 29:3, GNT

It is the vocation of all baptized Christians to become living icons, transparent windows through which the light of divine light pours. This is the ultimate search of human life, to become seers and bearers of that light.

© DAVID HAY JONES

Jesus said to John the Baptist, "God's work, putting things right all these centuries, is coming together right now in this baptism."

Matthew 3:15, THE MESSAGE

ISAIAH 42:1-9 · PSALM 29 ·
ACTS 10:34-43 · MATTHEW 3:13-17

How I love to do your will, my God! I
keep your teaching in my heart.

Psalm 40:8, GNT

God, who has called you into
fellowship with his Son Jesus Christ
our Lord, is faithful.

1 Corinthians 1:9, NIV

What is due me is in the LORD's hand,
and my reward is with my God.

Isaiah 49:4*b*, NIV

Now GOD, don't hold out on me, don't
hold back your passion. Your love and
truth are all that keeps me together.

Psalm 40:11, THE MESSAGE

[John the Baptist] saw Jesus coming toward him and declared, "Here is the Lamb of God who takes away the sin of the world!"

John 1:29, NRSV

John the Baptist said, "God . . . had said to me, 'You will see the Spirit come down and stay on a man; he is the one who baptizes with the Holy Spirit.'"

John 1:33, GNT

Love is the threshold where divine and human presence ebb and flow into each other.

JOHN O'DONOHUE

"I have seen it," said John, "and I tell you that he is the Son of God."

John 1:34, GNT

One thing I ask of the LORD, this is what I seek: that I may dwell in the house of the LORD all the days of my life.

Psalm 27:4, NIV

The people who walked in darkness have seen a great light; those who lived in a land of deep darkness—on them light has shined.

Isaiah 9:2, NRSV

The Message that points to Christ on the Cross seems like sheer silliness to those hellbent on destruction, but for those on the way of salvation it makes perfect sense.

1 Corinthians 1:18, THE MESSAGE

Paul wrote, "Christ did not send me to baptize but to proclaim the gospel, and not with eloquent wisdom, so that the cross of Christ might not be emptied of its power."

1 Corinthians 1:17, NRSV

Leaving Nazareth, [Jesus] went and
lived in Capernaum. . . . From that time
on [he] began to preach, "Repent, for
the kingdom of heaven is near."

Matthew 4:13, 17, NIV

Jesus said to [Peter and Andrew],
"Come with me, and I will teach you to
catch people."

Matthew 4:19, GNT

We tend to emphasize the distance between Jesus and ourselves. We see Jesus as the all-knowing and all-powerful Son of God who is unreachable for us sinful, broken human beings. But in thinking this way, we forget that Jesus came to . . . lift us up into loving community with the Father. Only when we recognize the radical purpose of Jesus' ministry will we be able to understand the meaning of the spiritual life.

HENRI J. M. NOUWEN

The LORD is my light and my salvation;
whom shall I fear?

Psalm 27:1, KJV

What [the LORD] requires of us is this:
to do what is just, to show constant
love, and to live in humble fellowship
with our God.

Micah 6:8, GNT

O LORD, who may abide in your tent?
Who may dwell on your holy hill?
Those who walk blamelessly, and do
what is right, and speak the truth from
their heart.

Psalm 15:1-2, NRSV

What seems to be God's foolishness is wiser than human wisdom, and what seems to be God's weakness is stronger than human strength.

I Corinthians 1:25, GNT

Jesus said, "Blessed are the poor in spirit: for theirs is the kingdom of heaven."

Matthew 5:3, KJV

God purposely chose what the world considers nonsense in order to shame the wise, and he chose what the world considers weak in order to shame the powerful.

1 Corinthians 1:27, GNT

Everything that we have—right thinking and right living, a clean slate and a fresh start—comes from God by way of Jesus Christ.

1 Corinthians 1:30, THE MESSAGE

We make the decision as to whether the events of our lives will serve as stepping stones or stumbling blocks.

MAXIE DUNNAM

Jesus said, "Blessed are the peacemakers,
for they will be called children of God."
Matthew 5:9, NRSV

The LORD says, "The kind of fasting I want is this: Remove the chains of oppression and the yoke of injustice, and let the oppressed go free."

Isaiah 58:6, GNT

Happy are those who fear the LORD, who greatly delight in his commandments.

Psalm 112:1, NRSV

The LORD *says,* "The kind of fasting I want is this: . . . Share your food with the hungry and open your homes to the homeless poor."

Isaiah 58:6, 7, GNT

Jesus said, "Your light must shine before people, so that they will see the good things you do and praise your Father in heaven."

Matthew 5:16, GNT

The LORD *says*, "The kind of fasting I want is this: . . . Give clothes to those who have nothing to wear, and do not refuse to help your own relatives."

Isaiah 58:6, 7, GNT

Paul wrote, "Your life of faith is a response to God's power, not to some fancy mental or emotional footwork by me or anyone else."

1 Corinthians 2:5, THE MESSAGE

In the winters of your prayer, when there seems to be nothing but darkness and a situation of general frozenness, hold on, wait for God. He will come.

© DAVID HAY JONES

The righteous will never be moved;
they will be remembered forever.

Psalm 112:6, NRSV

Moses said, "I have set before you today life and prosperity, death and adversity. If you obey the commandments of the LORD your God . . . , you shall live."

Deuteronomy 30:15-16, NRSV

Paul wrote, "We are partners working together for God, and you are God's field."

1 Corinthians 3:9, GNT

Happy are those whose way is
blameless, who walk in the law of
the LORD.

Psalm 119:1, NRSV

Jesus said, "Don't say anything you don't
mean. . . . You only make things worse
when you lay down a smoke screen of
pious talk, saying, 'I'll pray for you,' and
never doing it."

Matthew 5:33, THE MESSAGE

Neither the one who plants nor the one who waters is anything, but only God who gives the growth.

1 Corinthians 3:7, NRSV

Jesus said, "You don't make your words true by embellishing them with religious lace. In making your speech sound more religious, it becomes less true."

Matthew 5:36, THE MESSAGE

The life of the spirit is never static. We're born on one level, only to find some new struggle toward wholeness gestating within. That's the sacred intent of life, of God—to move us continuously toward growth, toward recovering all that is lost and orphaned within us and restoring the divine image imprinted on our soul.

SUE MONK KIDD

Jesus said, "If you enter your place of worship and, about to make an offering, you suddenly remember a grudge a friend has against you, abandon your offering . . . go to this friend and make things right."

Matthew 5:23-24, THE MESSAGE

Teach me, O LORD, the way of
thy statutes; and I shall keep it unto
the end.

Psalm 119:33, KJV

Jesus said, "Why should God reward you
if you love only the people who love
you? Even the tax collectors do that!"

Matthew 5:46, GNT

No one can lay any foundation other than the one already laid, which is Jesus Christ.

1 Corinthians 3:11, NIV

You should not fool yourself. If any of you think that you are wise by this world's standards, you should become a fool, in order to be really wise.

1 Corinthians 3:18, GNT

Jesus said, "You have heard that it was said, 'You shall love your neighbor and hate your enemy.' But I say to you, Love your enemies."

Matthew 5:43-44, NRSV

You belong to Christ, and Christ belongs to God.

1 Corinthians 3:23, GNT

I have come to understand that the voice of God is all around me. . . . God is speaking to me all the time. . . . I am only now beginning to listen, let alone to hear. In bare trees, I hear God saying that it is possible to die over and over again and yet survive.

JOAN CHITTISTER

Don't you know that you yourselves
are God's temple and that God's Spirit
lives in you?

1 Corinthians 3:16, NIV

For God alone my soul waits in silence,
for my hope is from him.

Psalm 62:5, NRSV

Jesus said, "You can't worship two gods
at once. Loving one god, you'll end
up hating the other. Adoration of one
feeds contempt for the other. You can't
worship God and Money both."

Matthew 6:24, THE MESSAGE

The LORD says, "Can a woman forget her own baby and not love the child she bore? Even if a mother should forget her child, I will never forget you."

Isaiah 49:15, GNT

Trust in [God] at all times, O people; pour out your heart before him; God is a refuge for us.

Psalm 62:8, NRSV

Jesus said, "Give your entire attention to what God is doing right now, and don't get worked up about what may or may not happen tomorrow."

Matthew 6:34, THE MESSAGE

Paul wrote, "Don't imagine us leaders to be something we aren't. We are servants of Christ, not his masters. We are guides into God's most sublime secrets, not security guards posted to protect them."

1 Corinthians 4:1, THE MESSAGE

Hope opens something in the human heart. Like shutters slowly parting to admit a winter dawn, hope permits strands of light to make their way to us, even when we stand in cold darkness; but hope also reveals a landscape beyond us into which we can live and move and have our being.

PAMELA HAWKINS

© DAVID HAY JONES

Sing, heavens! Shout for joy, earth! Let the mountains burst into song! The LORD will comfort his people.

Isaiah 49:13, GNT

Exalt the LORD our God and worship
at his holy mountain, for the LORD our
God is holy.

Psalm 99:9, NIV

The LORD said to Moses, "Come up to
me on the mountain, and wait there;
and I will give you the tablets of stone,
with the law and the commandment."

Exodus 24:12, NRSV

The appearance of the glory of the
LORD was like a devouring fire on the
top of the mountain in the sight of the
people of Israel.

Exodus 24:17, NRSV

Moses entered the cloud as he went on
up the mountain. And he stayed on the
mountain forty days and forty nights.

Exodus 24:18, NIV

Jesus took with him Peter and the brothers James and John and led them up a high mountain where they were alone.

Matthew 17:1, GNT

As they looked on, a change came over Jesus: his face was shining like the sun, and his clothes were dazzling white. Then the three disciples saw Moses and Elijah talking with Jesus.

Matthew 17:2-3, GNT

A tree gives glory to God by being a tree.

THOMAS MERTON

Peter wrote, "We have not depended on made-up stories in making known to you the mighty coming of our Lord Jesus Christ. With our own eyes we saw his greatness."

2 Peter 1:16, GNT

EXODUS 24:12-18 · PSALM 99 ·
2 PETER 1:16-21 · MATTHEW 17:1-9

Jesus answered [the devil] by quoting
Deuteronomy: "It takes more than
bread to stay alive. It takes a steady
stream of words from God's mouth."

Matthew 4:4, THE MESSAGE

The LORD *says,* "I will instruct you and
teach you in the way you should go; I
will counsel you and watch over you."

Psalm 32:8, NIV

ASH WEDNESDAY

Happy is the one whom the LORD does not accuse of doing wrong and who is free from all deceit.

Psalm 32:2, GNT

If one man's sin put crowds of people at the dead-end abyss of separation from God, just think what God's gift poured through one man, Jesus Christ, will do!

Romans 5:15, THE MESSAGE

More than just getting us out of trouble, [Christ] got us into life!

Romans 5:18, THE MESSAGE

Celebrate GOD. Sing together—everyone! All you honest hearts, raise the roof!

Psalm 32:11, THE MESSAGE

Transformation comes about when we are willing to admit God's word into our lives, to hear God's voice and to act upon it. . . . When I admit that God is in charge I am willing and ready to change.

ESTHER DE WAAL

FIRST SUNDAY IN LENT

Jesus said, "Go away, Satan! The scripture says, 'Worship the Lord your God and serve only him!'"

Matthew 4:10, GNT

GENESIS 2:15-17; 3:1-7 · PSALM 32 ·
ROMANS 5:12-19 · MATTHEW 4:1-11

The LORD said to Abram, "I will make of you a great nation, and I will bless you, and make your name great, so that you will be a blessing."

Genesis 12:2, NRSV

I lift up my eyes to the hills—from where will my help come? My help comes from the LORD, who made heaven and earth.

Psalm 121:1-2, NRSV

"I am telling you the truth," [said] Jesus, "that no one can enter the Kingdom of God without being born of water and the Spirit."

John 3:5, GNT

If what God promises is to be given to those who obey the Law, then faith means nothing.

Romans 4:14, GNT

GOD guards you from every evil, he guards your very life. He guards you when you leave and when you return, he guards you now, he guards you always.

Psalm 121:7-8, THE MESSAGE

Jesus said, "God so loved the world, that he gave his only begotten Son, that whosoever believeth in him should not perish, but have everlasting life."

John 3:16, KJV

When life goes dry, only the memory of God makes life bearable again.

JOAN CHITTISTER

When you know how much God is in love with you then you can only live your life radiating that love.

MOTHER TERESA

Let's march into [GOD's] presence singing praises, lifting the rafters with our hymns!

Psalm 95:2, THE MESSAGE

EXODUS 17:1-7 · PSALM 95 ·
ROMANS 5:1-11 · JOHN 4:5-42

The LORD does not see as mortals see;
they look on the outward appearance,
but the LORD looks on the heart.

1 Samuel 16:7*b*, NRSV

The Spirit of GOD entered David like
a rush of wind, God vitally empowering
him for the rest of his life.

1 Samuel 16:13, THE MESSAGE

Try to find out what is pleasing to the Lord. Take no part in the unfruitful works of darkness, but instead expose them.

Ephesians 5:10-11, NRSV

Jesus said, "While I am in the world, I am the light for the world."

John 9:5, GNT

The LORD is my shepherd; I shall
not want.

Psalm 23:1, KJV

The bright light of Christ makes your
way plain. So no more stumbling
around. Get on with it! The good, the
right, the true.

Ephesians 5:9, THE MESSAGE

Yours the seed, yours the growth;
yours the water, yours the thirst;
yours the wild, yours the tame.
You are within me, O God,
and within all creation—
and you are beyond.
Shape and fill me this day
and all creation
with your grace.

SAM HAMILTON-POORE

Surely goodness and mercy shall
follow me all the days of my life: and
I will dwell in the house of the LORD
for ever.

Psalm 23:6, KJV

Jesus said to [Martha], "I am the
resurrection and the life. Those who
believe in me, even though they die,
will live."

John 11:25, NRSV

Whoever does not have the Spirit of
Christ does not belong to him. But if
Christ lives in you, the Spirit is life for
you because you have been put right
with God.

Romans 8:9-10, GNT

From the depths of my despair I call to
you, LORD. Hear my cry, O Lord; listen
to my call for help!

Psalm 130:1-2, GNT

If you, O LORD, should mark iniquities,
Lord, who could stand? But there is
forgiveness with you.

Psalm 130:3-4, NRSV

I wait eagerly for the LORD's help,
and in his word I trust. I wait for the
Lord more eagerly than sentries wait
for the dawn.

Psalm 130:5-6, GNT

.

[Jesus] called out in a loud voice,
"Lazarus, come out!"

John 11:43, GNT

.

My *life flows on in endless song, above earth's lamentation.*
I hear the clear, though far-off hymn that hails a new creation.
No storm can shake my inmost calm while to that Rock I'm clinging.
Since love is Lord of heaven and earth,
How can I keep from singing?

ROBERT LOWRY

FIFTH SUNDAY IN LENT

[Lazarus] came out, his hands and feet wrapped in grave cloths, and with a cloth around his face. "Untie him," Jesus told them, "and let him go."

John 11:44, GNT

The stone that the builders rejected
has become the chief cornerstone.
This is the LORD's doing; it is
marvelous in our eyes.

Psalm 118:22-23, NRSV

The Master, GOD, has given me a
well-taught tongue, so I know how to
encourage tired people.

Isaiah 50:4, THE MESSAGE

This is the day which the LORD hath made; we will rejoice and be glad in it.

Psalm 118:24, KJV

The disciples went and did as Jesus had instructed them. They brought the donkey and the colt, placed their cloaks on them, and Jesus sat on them.

Matthew 21:6-7, NIV

Be merciful to me, O LORD, for I
am in distress; my eyes grow weak
with sorrow, my soul and my body
with grief.

Psalm 31:9, NIV

At the name of Jesus every knee should
bow, in heaven and on earth and under
the earth, and every tongue confess that
Jesus Christ is Lord.

Philippians 2:10-11, NIV

No particular Lenten journey is more perfect or right than another. Our journey to Easter is ours and no one else's. . . . Because we have adjusted our lives a little or a lot to follow Jesus through the ups and downs, the deserts and roads of Lent, . . . we will all find ourselves at a different place than where we began.

PAMELA HAWKINS

© DAVID HAY JONES

PASSION/PALM SUNDAY

Crowds went ahead [of Jesus] and crowds followed, all of them calling out, "Hosanna to David's son!" "Blessed is he who comes in God's name!" "Hosanna in highest heaven!"

Matthew 21:9, THE MESSAGE

Jesus said, "You always have the poor with you, but you do not always have me."

John 12:8, NRSV

Jesus said, "My soul is troubled. And what should I say—'Father, save me from this hour'? No, it is for this reason that I have come to this hour. Father, glorify your name."

John 12:27-28, NRSV

The scriptures for this week are from the daily lections for Holy Week.

[Jesus] was deeply troubled and declared openly, "I am telling you the truth: one of you is going to betray me."

John 13:21, GNT

MAUNDY THURSDAY

[Jesus] poured some water into a washbasin and began to wash the disciples' feet and dry them with the towel around his waist.

John 13:5, GNT

GOOD FRIDAY

Jesus said, "It is finished." With that, he bowed his head and gave up his spirit.

John 19:30, NIV

HOLY SATURDAY

We know that our old being has been put to death with Christ on his cross, in order that the power of the sinful self might be destroyed, so that we should no longer be the slaves of sin.

Romans 6:6, GNT

Near the cross! O Lamb of God,
bring its scenes before me;
Help me walk from day to day
with its shadow o'er me.

In the cross, in the cross,
be my glory ever,
Till my raptured soul shall find
rest beyond the river.

FANNY CROSBY

EASTER DAY

The angel spoke to the women: "There is nothing to fear here. I know you're looking for Jesus, the One they nailed to the cross. He is not here. He was raised, just as he said."

Matthew 28:5-6, THE MESSAGE

You have made known to me the path of life [O God]; you will fill me with joy in your presence, with eternal pleasures at your right hand.

Psalm 16:11, NIV

Let us give thanks to the God and Father of our Lord Jesus Christ! Because of his great mercy he gave us new life by raising Jesus Christ from death.

1 Peter 1:3, GNT

Jesus came and stood among [the disciples] and said, "Peace be with you." After he said this, he showed them his hands and his side.

John 20:19-20, NRSV

I say to the LORD, "You are my Lord; all the good things I have come from you."

Psalm 16:2, GNT

When Jesus wraps this all up, it's your
faith, not your gold, that God will have
on display as evidence of his victory.

1 Peter 1:7, THE MESSAGE

God untied the death ropes and raised
[Jesus] up. Death was no match for
him. David said it all: I saw God before
me for all time.

Acts 2:24-25, THE MESSAGE

Taking off your shoes is a sacred ritual. . . . Whether you take off your shoes symbolically or literally matters little. What is important is that you are alive to the holy ground *on which* you stand *and to the* holy ground *that you are.*

MACRINA WIEDERKEHR

[Jesus] breathed on [the disciples] and said to them, "Receive the Holy Spirit."

John 20:22, NRSV

ACTS 2:14A, 22-32 · PSALM 16 ·
I PETER 1:3-9 · JOHN 20:19-31

I love the LORD, for he heard my voice;
he heard my cry for mercy.

Psalm 116:1, NIV

Through [Christ] you believe in God,
who raised him from death and gave
him glory; and so your faith and hope
are fixed on God.

1 Peter 1:21, GNT

Peter said to [the crowd at Pentecost], "Each one of you must turn away from your sins and be baptized in the name of Jesus Christ, so that your sins will be forgiven."

Acts 2:38, GNT

Now that you've cleaned up your lives by following the truth, love one another as if your lives depended on it.

1 Peter 1:22, THE MESSAGE

[Jesus] sat down at the table with them. Taking the bread, he blessed and broke and gave it to them. At that moment, open-eyed, wide-eyed, they recognized him.

Luke 24:30-31, THE MESSAGE

Back and forth they talked. "Didn't we feel on fire as [Jesus] conversed with us on the road, as he opened up the Scriptures for us?"

Luke 24:32, THE MESSAGE

When our heads are up and our eyes wide open, we see the grandeur of God flaming out from every seed and stone, and the image of God shining in every human face.

SUSAN BRIEHL

I will pay my vows unto the LORD now
in the presence of all his people.

Psalm 116:18, KJV

[The LORD] gives me new strength.
He guides me in the right paths, as he
has promised.

Psalm 23:3, GNT

Even when the way goes through Death
Valley, I'm not afraid when you [GOD]
walk at my side.

Psalm 23:4, THE MESSAGE

Jesus said, "I am the gate. Whoever enters by me will be saved, and will come in and go out and find pasture."

John 10:9, NRSV

[The new followers of Christ] devoted themselves to the apostles' teaching and fellowship, to the breaking of bread and the prayers.

Acts 2:42, NRSV

Day by day the Lord added to their number those who were being saved.

Acts 2:47, NRSV

If you endure suffering even when you have done right, God will bless you for it.

1 Peter 2:20*b*, GNT

Faithful discipleship includes fidelity and loving attention to our closest relationships. . . .
Close relationships offer us special opportunity to grow in faithfulness precisely because they
challenge us over long periods of time.

MARY LOU REDDING

You were like sheep that had lost their way, but now you have been brought back to follow the Shepherd and Keeper of your souls.

1 Peter 2:25, GNT

Jesus said, "Do not let your hearts be troubled. Believe in God, believe also in me."

John 14:1, NRSV

Come to the Lord, the living stone rejected by people as worthless but chosen by God as valuable.

1 Peter 2:4, GNT

Jesus said, "If you know me, you will know my Father also. From now on you do know him and have seen him."

John 14:7, NRSV

Stephen prayed, "Master Jesus, take my life." Then he knelt down, praying loud enough for everyone to hear, "Master, don't blame them for this sin"—his last words. Then he died.

Acts 7:59-60, THE MESSAGE

Into your hands I commit my spirit;
redeem me, O LORD, the God of truth.

Psalm 31:5, NIV

Jesus said, "If I go and prepare a place for
you, I will come again and will take you
to myself, so that where I am, there you
may be also."

John 14:3, NRSV

It is better to suffer for doing good, if
suffering should be God's will, than to
suffer for doing evil.

1 Peter 3:17, NRSV

[God] has set a day when the entire
human race will be judged and
everything set right. And he has already
appointed the judge, confirming him
before everyone by raising him from
the dead.

Acts 17:31, THE MESSAGE

God is everywhere
utterly vast,
and everywhere near at hand,
according to his own witness of himself;
I am, he says, a God at hand
and not a God afar off.
The God we are seeking
is not one who dwells far away from us;
we have him within us.

SAINT COLUMBANUS

Jesus said, "I will ask the Father, and he will give you another Helper, who will stay with you forever. He is the Spirit, who reveals the truth about God."

John 14:16-17*a*, GNT

Sing to God, sing praises to his name;
prepare a way for him who rides on the
clouds. His name is the LORD—be glad
in his presence!

Psalm 68:4, GNT

Rejoice that you participate in the
sufferings of Christ, so that you may be
overjoyed when his glory is revealed.

1 Peter 4:13, NIV

Jesus said to the apostles, "You will receive power when the Holy Spirit has come upon you; and you will be my witnesses . . . to the ends of the earth."

Acts 1:8, NRSV

As [the apostles] were watching, [Jesus] was lifted up, and a cloud took him out of their sight.

Acts 1:9, NRSV

Cast all your anxiety on [God] because he cares for you.

1 Peter 5:7, NIV

Jesus prayed to his Father, "I spelled out your character in detail to the men and women you gave me. . . . And they have now done what you said."

John 17:6, THE MESSAGE

To cling always to God and to the things of God—this must be our major effort, this must be the road that the heart follows unswervingly.

JOHN CASSIAN

Jesus prayed, "Now I am coming to you; I am no longer in the world, but [my followers] are in the world. Holy Father! Keep them safe by the power of your name."

John 17:11, GNT

MONDAY · JUNE 6

Oh, let me sing to GOD all my life long,
sing hymns to my God as long as I live!
Psalm 104:33, THE MESSAGE

TUESDAY · JUNE 7

Jesus said, "Let anyone who is thirsty
come to me."
John 7:37, NRSV

This is what I will do in the last days,
God says: I will pour out my Spirit
on everyone.

Acts 2:17*a*, GNT

There are different kinds of gifts, but
the same Spirit. There are different
kinds of service, but the same Lord.

1 Corinthians 12:4-5, NIV

The body is a unit, though it is made up of many parts; and though all its parts are many, they form one body. So it is with Christ.

1 Corinthians 12:12, NIV

In the one Spirit we were all baptized into one body . . . and we were all made to drink of one Spirit.

1 Corinthians 12:13, NRSV

God is the friend of silence—we need to listen to God because it's not what we say but what He says to us and through us that matters.

MOTHER TERESA

PENTECOST

[The believers] were all filled with the Holy Spirit and began to talk in other languages, as the Spirit enabled them to speak.

Acts 2:4, GNT

[O LORD], when I look at the sky, which you have made, at the moon and the stars, which you set in their places—what are human beings, that you think of them?

Psalm 8:3-4, GNT

Jesus said, "All authority in heaven and on earth has been given to me. Go therefore and make disciples of all nations."

Matthew 28:18-19, NRSV

God created human beings; he created
them godlike, reflecting God's nature.

Genesis 1:27, THE MESSAGE

[O LORD], you made [human beings]
inferior only to yourself; you crowned
them with glory and honor.

Psalm 8:5, GNT

Paul wrote, "Now, my friends, good-bye! Strive for perfection; listen to my appeals; agree with one another; live in peace. And the God of love and peace will be with you."

2 Corinthians 13:11, GNT

Jesus said, "Remember, I am with you always, to the end of the age."

Matthew 28:20, NRSV

Get close to the earth. Walk whenever you can. Listen to the birds.
Enjoy the texture of grass and leaves. Smell the flowers. Marvel in the
rich colors everywhere. Simplicity means to discover once again that
"the earth is the LORD's and the fullness thereof" (Ps. 24:1).

RICHARD J. FOSTER

The amazing grace of the Master, Jesus
Christ, the extravagant love of God, the
intimate friendship of the Holy Spirit,
be with all of you.

2 Corinthians 13:14, THE MESSAGE

I will sing to you, O LORD, because you have been good to me.

Psalm 13:6, GNT

Sin can't tell you how to live. After all, you're not living under that old tyranny any longer. You're living in the freedom of God.

Romans 6:14, THE MESSAGE

Jesus said, "Whoever welcomes you welcomes me, and whoever welcomes me welcomes the one who sent me."

Matthew 10:40, NRSV

How much longer will you forget me, LORD? Forever? How much longer will you hide yourself from me?

Psalm 13:1, GNT

The wages of sin is death, but the free gift of God is eternal life in Christ Jesus our Lord.

Romans 6:23, NRSV

Jesus said, "Accepting a messenger of God is as good as being God's messenger. Accepting someone's help is as good as giving someone help."

Matthew 10:41, THE MESSAGE

Embracing the Sabbath helps us stand against pride. It helps us set aside our worship of our own achievements for one day each week and helps us know deep inside that the world is God's.

LYNNE BABB

Look at me, O LORD my God, and answer me. Restore my strength.

Psalm 13:3, GNT

Paul wrote, "I do not understand what I do; for I don't do what I would like to do, but instead I do what I hate."

Romans 7:15, GNT

Praise be to the LORD God, the God of Israel, who alone does marvelous deeds.

Psalm 72:18, NIV

Jesus said, "No one knows the Son except the Father, and no one knows the Father except the Son and those to whom the Son chooses to reveal him."

Matthew 11:27, NIV

Paul wrote, "Who will rescue me from this body that is taking me to death? Thanks be to God, who does this through our Lord Jesus Christ!"

Romans 7:24-25, GNT

Paul wrote, "I truly delight in God's commands, but it's pretty obvious that not all of me joins in that delight. Parts of me covertly rebel."

Romans 7:22-23, THE MESSAGE

Jesus said, "Are you tired? Worn out? Burned out on religion? Come to me. Get away with me and you'll recover your life."

Matthew 11:28, THE MESSAGE

If you wish to know a good fruit and plant, you must touch and taste it and then you know it. So too it is with Christ, the tree of life. Taste and touch in faith his humility, meekness, and patience; eat of his fruit and you will find rest for your soul.

JOHANN ARNDT

Jesus said, "Take my yoke upon you, and learn of me; for I am meek and lowly in heart: and ye shall find rest unto your souls."

Matthew 11:29, KJV

Paul wrote, "The law of the Spirit, which brings us life in union with Christ Jesus, has set me free from the law of sin and death."

Romans 8:2, GNT

To you, O LORD, I offer my prayer; in you, my God, I trust.

Psalm 25:1-2*a*, GNT

Your word [O LORD] is a lamp to my
feet and a light to my path.

Psalm 119:105, NRSV

Those who trust God's action in them
find that God's Spirit is in them—living
and breathing God!

Romans 8:5, THE MESSAGE

There is now no condemnation for those who are in Christ Jesus.

Romans 8:1, NIV

Focusing on the self is the opposite of focusing on God.

Romans 8:7, THE MESSAGE

The elevator that must lift me up to heaven is Your arms, Jesus! For that I do not need to become big. On the contrary, I have to stay little—may I become little, more and more.

THÉRÈSE OF LISIEUX

Such large crowds gathered around [Jesus] that he got into a boat and sat in it, while all the people stood on the shore. Then he told them many things in parables.

Matthew 13:2-3, NIV

The LORD *said to Jacob,* "I am the
LORD, the God of Abraham your father
and the God of Isaac; the land on
which you lie I will give to you and to
your offspring."

Genesis 28:13, NRSV

Jacob woke from his sleep and said,
"Surely the LORD is in this place—and I
did not know it!"

Genesis 28:16, NRSV

Those who are led by God's Spirit are God's children.

Romans 8:14, GNT

Since we are [God's] children, we will possess . . . with Christ what God has kept for him; for if we share Christ's suffering, we will also share his glory.

Romans 8:17, GNT

Paul wrote, "I consider that what we suffer at this present time cannot be compared at all with the glory that is going to be revealed to us."

Romans 8:18, GNT

Search me, O God, and know my heart: try me, and know my thoughts: And see if there be any wicked way in me, and lead me in the way everlasting.

Psalm 139:23-24, KJV

Rhythm is the secret key to balance and belonging. . . . When you are in rhythm with your nature, nothing destructive can touch you. Providence is at one with you; it minds you and brings you to your new horizons. To be spiritual is to be in rhythm.

JOHN O'DONOHUE

[Jacob] said, "How awesome is this place! This is none other than the house of God, and this is the gate of heaven."

Genesis 28:17, NRSV

Thank GOD! Pray to him by name! Tell everyone you meet what he has done!

Psalm 105:1, THE MESSAGE

The Spirit helps us in our weakness; for we do not know how to pray as we ought, but that very Spirit intercedes with sighs too deep for words.

Romans 8:26, NRSV

Keep your eyes open for GOD,
watch for his works; be alert for signs
of his presence.

Psalm 105:4, THE MESSAGE

If God is for us, who can be against us?

Romans 8:31b, GNT

Paul wrote, "I am certain that nothing can separate us from [God's] love: neither death nor life, neither angels nor other heavenly rulers or powers, neither the present nor the future."

Romans 8:38, GNT

[GOD] remembers his Covenant—for a thousand generations he's been as good as his word.

Psalm 105:8, THE MESSAGE

Allowing ourselves to mourn develops our capacity to feel life's joys. . . . As we learn to feel all of our feelings, we explore what it means to be fully human, to be all that God created us to be.

MARY LOU REDDING

We know that in all things God works
for the good of those who love him.

Romans 8:28, NIV

A lot of people from the nearby villages walked around the lake to where [Jesus] was. When he saw them coming, he was overcome with pity and healed their sick.

Matthew 14:14, THE MESSAGE

I pray to you, O God, because you answer me; so turn to me and listen to my words.

Psalm 17:6, GNT

May God, who rules over all, be
praised forever!

Romans 9:5*b*, GNT

[The man who wrestled with Jacob]
said, "Your name is no longer Jacob.
From now on it's Israel (God-
Wrestler); you've wrestled with God
and you've come through."

Genesis 32:28, THE MESSAGE

Jacob named the place Peniel (God's Face) because, he said, "I saw God face-to-face and lived to tell the story!"

Genesis 32:30, THE MESSAGE

Hear, O LORD, my righteous plea; listen to my cry. Give ear to my prayer—it does not rise from deceitful lips.

Psalm 17:1, NIV

Prayer and love are really learned in the hour when prayer becomes impossible and your heart turns to stone.

THOMAS MERTON

[Jesus] lifted his face to heaven in prayer, blessed, broke, and gave the bread to the disciples. The disciples then gave the food to the congregation. They all ate their fill.

Matthew 14:19-20, THE MESSAGE

GENESIS 32:22-31 · PSALM 17:1-7, 15 ·
ROMANS 9:1-5 · MATTHEW 14:13-21

Sing [GOD] songs, belt out hymns,
translate his wonders into music!
Honor his holy name with Hallelujahs,
you who seek GOD.

Psalm 105:2-3, THE MESSAGE

There is no distinction between Jew
and Greek; the same Lord is Lord of all
and is generous to all who call on him.

Romans 10:12, NRSV

After sending the people away, [Jesus]
went up a hill by himself to pray.

Matthew 14:23, GNT

Between three and six o'clock in the
morning Jesus came to the disciples,
walking on the water.

Matthew 14:25, GNT

When [Peter] saw the wind, he was afraid and, beginning to sink, cried out, "Lord, save me!"

Matthew 14:30, NIV

Immediately Jesus reached out his hand and caught [Peter]. "You of little faith," he said, "why did you doubt?"

Matthew 14:31, NIV

God said to the soul:
I desired you before the world began.
I desire you now
As you desire me.
And where the desires of two come together
There love is perfected.

MECHTHILD OF MAGDEBURG

© DAVID HAY JONES

The scripture says, "Everyone who calls out to the Lord for help will be saved."

Romans 10:13, GNT

How wonderful it is, how pleasant, for
God's people to live together
in harmony!

Psalm 133:1, GNT

Jesus said, "Listen and understand: it
is not what goes into the mouth that
defiles a person, but it is what comes
out of the mouth that defiles."

Matthew 15:10-11, NRSV

God does not change his mind about
whom he chooses and blesses.

Romans 11:29, GNT

Jesus told his disciples, "Forget [the
Pharisees]. They are blind men
leading blind men. When a blind man
leads a blind man, they both end up in
the ditch."

Matthew 15:14, THE MESSAGE

In one way or another, God makes sure
that we all experience what it means
to be outside so that he can personally
open the door and welcome us back in.

Romans 11:32, THE MESSAGE

Jesus said, "Every plant that my
heavenly Father has not planted
will be uprooted."

Matthew 15:13, NRSV

Faith comes and goes. It rises and falls like the tides of an invisible ocean. If it is presumptuous to think that faith will stay with you forever, it is just as presumptuous to think that unbelief will.

FLANNERY O'CONNOR

The woman came and knelt before
[Jesus]. "Lord, help me!" she said. . .
Jesus answered, "Woman, you have
great faith! Your request is granted."

Matthew 15:25, 28, NIV

Oh, blessed be GOD! He didn't go off
and leave us. . . . GOD's strong name
is our help, the same GOD who made
heaven and earth.

Psalm 124:6, 8, THE MESSAGE

Paul wrote, "I appeal to you therefore,
brothers and sisters, by the mercies of
God, to present your bodies as a living
sacrifice, holy and acceptable to God,
which is your spiritual worship."

Romans 12:1, NRSV

"What about you?" [Jesus] asked [the disciples]. "Who do you say I am?" Simon Peter answered, "You are the Messiah, the Son of the living God."

Matthew 16:15-16, GNT

Jesus said, "I tell you, Peter: you are a rock, and on this rock foundation I will build my church, and not even death will ever be able to overcome it."

Matthew 16:18, GNT

Don't become so well-adjusted to your culture that you fit into it without even thinking. Instead, fix your attention on God. You'll be changed from the inside out.

Romans 12:2, THE MESSAGE

Do not think of yourself more highly than you should. Instead, be modest in your thinking, and judge yourself according to the amount of faith that God has given you.

Romans 12:3, GNT

None of us can describe God, exactly, but we know when we have God moments. . . . They are moments of recognition when we know what is true, realize what is real, and experience what is good. God moments are rare glimpses into eternity.

JEREMY LANGFORD

© DAVID HAY JONES

In Christ we who are many form one body, and each member belongs to all the others.

Romans 12:5, NIV

The angel of the LORD appeared to
[Moses] in a flame of fire out of a bush;
he looked, and the bush was blazing, yet
it was not consumed.

Exodus 3:2, NRSV

Moses said to God, "Who am I that
I should go to Pharaoh, and bring the
Israelites out of Egypt?" [God] said, "I
will be with you."

Exodus 3:11-12, NRSV

Jesus said to his disciples, "If you want to save your own life, you will lose it; but if you lose your life for my sake, you will find it."

Matthew 16:25, GNT

Paul wrote, "Love must be sincere. Hate what is evil; cling to what is good."

Romans 12:9, NIV

Jesus said, "Will you gain anything if you win the whole world but lose your life?"

Matthew 16:26, GNT

Paul wrote, "Do not take revenge, my friends, but leave room for God's wrath, for it is written: 'It is mine to avenge: I will repay,' says the Lord."

Romans 12:19, NIV

Forgiveness is a gift, God's gift, first of all, to each of us. And then a gift we give to others, a gift that, in the giving, brings to the giver unexpected and undeniable blessing.

KENNETH GIBBLE

Paul quoted from Proverbs, "If your enemy is hungry, feed him; if he is thirsty, give him something to drink. In doing this, you will heap burning coals on his head."

Romans 12:20, NIV

EXODUS 3:1-15 · PSALM 105:1-6, 23-26, 45C ·
ROMANS 12:9-21 · MATTHEW 16:21-28

The LORD takes pleasure in his people;
he honors the humble with victory.

Psalm 149:4, GNT

Owe no one anything, except to love
one another; for the one who loves
another has fulfilled the law.

Romans 13:8, NRSV

Jesus said, "Whenever two of you on earth agree about anything you pray for, it will be done for you by my Father in heaven."

Matthew 18:19, GNT

Jesus said, "Where two or three come together in my name, I am there with them."

Matthew 18:20, GNT

You can't go wrong when you love
others. When you add up everything in
the law code, the sum total is *love*.

Romans 13:10, THE MESSAGE

Let us put aside the deeds of darkness
and put on the armor of light.

Romans 13:12, NIV

The fact is that you're surrounded by God and you don't see God, because you "know" about God. The final barrier to the vision of God is your God concept. You miss God because you think you know.

ANTHONY DE MELLO

Hallelujah! Sing to GOD a brand-new song, praise him in the company of all who love him.

Psalm 149:1, THE MESSAGE

Peter asked Jesus, "Master, how many times do I forgive a brother or sister who hurts me? Seven?" Jesus replied, "Seven! Hardly. Try seventy times seven."

Matthew 18:21-22, THE MESSAGE

The angel of God who was going before the Israelite army moved and went behind them; and the pillar of cloud moved from in front of them and took its place behind them.

Exodus 14:19, NRSV

The Israelites walked on dry ground through the sea, the waters forming a wall for them on their right and on their left. Thus the LORD saved Israel that day.

Exodus 14:29-30, NRSV

Moses and the Israelites sang this song to the LORD: "I will sing to the LORD, for he is highly exalted. . . . The LORD is my strength and my song; he has become my salvation."

Exodus 15:1-2, NIV

Welcome those who are weak in faith,
but do not argue with them about their
personal opinions.

Romans 14:1, GNT

If we live, it is for the Lord that we live,
and if we die, it is for the Lord that
we die. So whether we live or die, we
belong to the Lord.

Romans 14:8, GNT

The important thing is that your way of life should be as the gospel of Christ requires.

Philippians 1:27, GNT

You have been given the privilege of serving Christ, not only by believing in him, but also by suffering for him.

Philippians 1:29, GNT

Sometimes it is only nature that revives me. I say to myself: There must be purpose in all of this. If this can exist, can bring beauty, can bring shelter, can bring new life, then so may I exist for a purpose beyond me.

JOAN CHITTISTER

Give ear, O my people, to my teaching; incline your ears to the words of my mouth.

Psalm 78:1, NRSV

The Israelites complained and put the LORD to the test when they asked, "Is the LORD with us or not?"

Exodus 17:7, GNT

[Jesus] was back in the Temple, teaching. The high priests and leaders of the people came up and demanded, "Show us your credentials. Who authorized you to teach here?"

Matthew 21:23, THE MESSAGE

Your life in Christ makes you strong, and his love comforts you. You have fellowship with the Spirit, and you have kindness and compassion for one another.

Philippians 2:1, GNT

Don't be obsessed with getting your own advantage. Forget yourselves long enough to lend a helping hand.

Philippians 2:4, THE MESSAGE

God is always at work in you to
make you willing and able to obey his
own purpose.

Philippians 2:13, GNT

Jesus said to the chief priests and elders, "The
tax collectors and the prostitutes are
entering the kingdom of God ahead of
you. For John came to you to show you
the way of righteousness, and you did
not believe him."

Matthew 21:31-32, NIV

We are not made for the mountains, for sunrises, or for the other beautiful attractions in life—those are simply intended to be moments of inspiration. We are made for the valley and the ordinary things of life, and that is where we have to prove our stamina and strength.

OSWALD CHAMBERS

In honor of the name of Jesus all beings in heaven, on earth, and in the world below will fall on their knees, and all will openly proclaim that Jesus Christ is Lord.

Philippians 2:10-11, GNT

The laws of the LORD are right, and
those who obey them are happy.

Psalm 19:8*a*, GNT

Paul wrote, "All I want is to know
Christ and to experience the power of
his resurrection."

Philippians 3:10, GNT

The heavens declare the glory of
God; the skies proclaim the work of
his hands.

Psalm 19:1, NIV

Paul wrote, "I've got my eye on the goal,
where God is beckoning us onward—to
Jesus. I'm off and running, and I'm not
turning back."

Philippians 3:14, THE MESSAGE

Paul wrote, "I now have the righteousness that is given through faith in Christ, the righteousness that comes from God and is based on faith."

Philippians 3:9c, GNT

Remember the sabbath day, and keep it holy.

Exodus 20:8, NRSV

Glory to you, my Lord, for sister water
Who is very useful and humble
And precious and pure.

FRANCIS OF ASSISI

Let the words of my mouth and
the meditation of my heart be
acceptable to you, O LORD, my rock
and my redeemer.

Psalm 19:14, NRSV

The king in Jesus' parable said, "The wedding banquet is ready, but those I invited did not deserve to come. Go to the street corners and invite to the banquet anyone you find."

Matthew 22:8-9, NIV

Hallelujah! Thank GOD! And why? Because he's good, because his love lasts.

Psalm 106:1, THE MESSAGE

Do not worry about anything, but in everything by prayer and supplication with thanksgiving let your requests be made known to God.

Philippians 4:6, NRSV

The peace of God, which surpasses all understanding, will guard your hearts and your minds in Christ Jesus.

Philippians 4:7, NRSV

Happy are those who obey [the LORD's] commands, who always do what is right.

Psalm 106:3, GNT

When God said that he would destroy his people, his chosen servant, Moses, stood up against God and kept his anger from destroying them.

Psalm 106:23, GNT

Do not worry about the tensions and struggles in your life, because the same loving Father who takes care of you today will take care of you tomorrow.

SAINT FRANCIS DE SALES

Paul wrote, "Rejoice in the Lord always; again I will say, Rejoice."
Philippians 4:4, NRSV

Jesus said to the Pharisees, "Pay to the Emperor what belongs to the Emperor, and pay to God what belongs to God."

Matthew 22:21, GNT

The LORD said to Moses, "I will be gracious to whom I will be gracious, and will show mercy on whom I will show mercy."

Exodus 33:19, NRSV

Paul wrote, "Even though you suffered much, you received the message with the joy that comes from the Holy Spirit."

1 Thessalonians 1:6*b*, GNT

The LORD reigns, let the nations tremble.

Psalm 99:1, NIV

GOD said [to Moses], "My presence will go with you. I'll see the journey to the end."

Exodus 33:14, THE MESSAGE

Lift high GOD, our God; worship at his holy mountain. Holy. Yes, holy is GOD our God.

Psalm 99:9, THE MESSAGE

The greatest gift one can give is thanksgiving. In giving gifts, we give what we can spare, but in giving thanks we give ourselves.

DAVID STEINDL-RAST

Paul wrote, "We always thank God for you all and always mention you in our prayers."
1 Thessalonians 1:2, GNT

Moses, the LORD's servant, died there in the land of Moab, as the LORD had said he would.

Deuteronomy 34:5, GNT

Paul wrote, "Be assured that when we speak to you we're not after crowd approval—only God approval."

1 Thessalonians 2:4, THE MESSAGE

Surprise us with love at daybreak [O God]; then we'll skip and dance all the day long.

Psalm 90:14, THE MESSAGE

There has never been a prophet in Israel like Moses; the LORD spoke with him face-to-face.

Deuteronomy 34:10, GNT

Jesus said, "Love the Lord your God with all your heart, with all your soul, and with all your mind. This is the greatest and the most important commandment."

Matthew 22:37-38, GNT

Jesus said, "The second most important commandment is [this]: 'Love your neighbor as you love yourself.' The whole Law of Moses and the teachings of the prophets depend on these two commandments."

Matthew 22:39-40, GNT

The Lord asks only two things of us:
Love for [God] and love for our neighbor. . . .
We cannot be sure if we are loving God, . . .
but we can know quite well if we are loving our neighbor.

TERESA OF AVILA

God, it seems you've been our home forever; long before the mountains were born, long before you brought earth itself to birth, from "once upon a time" to "kingdom come"—you are God.

Psalm 90:1-2, THE MESSAGE

The LORD said to Joshua, "Today I will begin to exalt you in the eyes of all Israel, so they may know that I am with you as I was with Moses."

Joshua 3:7, NIV

O give thanks unto the LORD, for he is good: for his mercy endureth for ever.

Psalm 107:1, KJV

Paul wrote, "We encouraged you, we comforted you, and we kept urging you to live the kind of life that pleases God."

1 Thessalonians 2:12, GNT

Paul wrote, "When we brought you God's message, you heard it and accepted it, not as a message from human beings but as God's message, which indeed it is."

1 Thessalonians 2:13, GNT

In your desperate condition, you called out to GOD. He got you out in the nick of time.

Psalm 107:6, THE MESSAGE

Jesus said, "The greatest one among you must be your servant."

Matthew 23:11, GNT

Autumn trees ask me not to worry. They, like Jesus, suggest trust rather than worry. So often in autumn I want to go lean my head against a tree and ask what it feels like to lose so much, to be so empty, so detached, . . . and then simply to stand and wait for God's refilling. . . . It isn't easy. But it's possible.

MACRINA WIEDERKEHR

Jesus said, "All who exalt themselves
will be humbled, and all who humble
themselves will be exalted."

Matthew 23:12, NRSV

[The LORD] instructed our ancestors
to teach his laws to their children. . . .
In this way they also will put their trust
in God.

Psalm 78:5, 7, GNT

Since we believe that Jesus died
and rose again, even so, through Jesus,
God will bring with him those who
have died.

1 Thessalonians 4:14, NRSV

Those who have died believing in Christ will rise to life first.

1 Thessalonians 4:16, GNT

We who are living [at the time Christ appears] will be gathered up . . . to meet the Lord in the air. And so we will always be with the Lord.

1 Thessalonians 4:17, GNT

Fear GOD. Worship him in total commitment.

Joshua 24:14, THE MESSAGE

Keep watch, because you do not know the day or the hour [of the Lord's coming].

Matthew 25:13, NIV

To be a saint does not mean never to sin. It means to start again with humility and joy after each fall.

DOM HELDER CÂMARA

ALL SAINTS SUNDAY

Joshua said, "If you decide that it's a bad thing to worship GOD, then choose a god you'd rather serve—and do it today. . . . As for me and my family, we'll worship GOD.

Joshua 24;15, THE MESSAGE

Our eyes look to the LORD our God,
until he has mercy upon us.

Psalm 123:2, NRSV

Encourage one another and help one
another, just as you are now doing.

1 Thessalonians 5:11, GNT

You yourselves know very well that the Day of the Lord will come as a thief comes at night.

1 Thessalonians 5:2, GNT

Do for GOD what you said you'd do—he is, after all, your God.

Psalm 76:11, THE MESSAGE

We must wear faith and love as a
breastplate, and our hope of salvation
as a helmet.

1 Thessalonians 5:8, GNT

God did not choose us to suffer his
anger, but to possess salvation through
our Lord Jesus Christ.

1 Thessalonians 5:9, GNT

Let us fly, fly away home into the depths of our souls where God awaits, . . . where we are always welcome, always awaited, where we hear and recognize our mother tongue.

JOHN KIRVAN

[Christ] died for us in order that we
might live together with him, whether
we are alive or dead when he comes.

1 Thessalonians 5:10, GNT

JUDGES 4:1-7 · PSALM 123 OR PSALM 76 ·
1 THESSALONIANS 5:1-11 · MATTHEW 25:14-30

Shout for joy to the LORD, all the earth.
Worship the LORD with gladness; come
before him with joyful songs.

Psalm 100:1-2, NIV

Paul wrote, "Ever since I heard of your
faith in the Lord Jesus and your love for
all of God's people, I have not stopped
giving thanks to God for you."

Ephesians 1:15-16a, GNT

This power working in us is the same as the mighty strength which [God] used when he raised Christ from death.

Ephesians 1:19-20, GNT

Know that the LORD is God. It is he that made us, and we are his.

Psalm 100:3, NRSV

The Sovereign LORD says, "I myself will search for my sheep and look after them."

Ezekiel 34:11, NIV

The King will say, "I'm telling the solemn truth: Whenever you did one of these [acts of compassion] to someone overlooked or ignored, that was me—you did it to me."

Matthew 25:40, THE MESSAGE

Every single creature is full of God and is a book about God.

MEISTER ECKHART

REIGN OF CHRIST SUNDAY

The church is Christ's body, in which he speaks and acts, by which he fills everything with his presence.

Ephesians 1:23, THE MESSAGE

EZEKIEL 34:11-16, 20-24 · PSALM 100 ·
EPHESIANS 1:15-23 · MATTHEW 25:31-46

MONDAY · NOVEMBER **21**

Restore us, O God; let your face shine, that we may be saved.

Psalm 80:3, NRSV

TUESDAY · NOVEMBER **22**

No one has ever seen or heard of a God like you, who does such [powerful] deeds for those who put their hope in him.

Isaiah 64:4, GNT

May God our Father and the Lord
Jesus Christ give you grace and peace.

1 Corinthians 1:3, GNT

THANKSGIVING DAY

God is to be trusted, the God who
called you to have fellowship with his
Son Jesus Christ, our Lord.

1 Corinthians 1:9, GNT

You come to the help of those who
gladly do right [O LORD], who
remember your ways.

Isaiah 64:5, NIV

O LORD, you are our Father. We are
the clay, you are the potter; we are all
the work of your hand.

Isaiah 64:8, NIV

The birth of Christ in our souls is for a purpose beyond ourselves: it is because his manifestation in the world must be through us. Every Christian is . . . part of the dust-laden air which shall radiate the glowing epiphany of God, catch and reflect his golden Light.

EVELYN UNDERHILL

© DAVID HAY JONES

FIRST SUNDAY OF ADVENT

Jesus said, "Heaven and earth will pass away, but my words will never pass away."

Mark 13:31, GNT

The glory of the LORD shall be
revealed, and all people shall see
it together.

Isaiah 40:5, NRSV

The prophet Isaiah said, "Prepare for
God's arrival! Make the road smooth
and straight!"

Mark 1:3, THE MESSAGE

John appeared in the desert,
baptizing and preaching. "Turn away
from your sins and be baptized," he
told the people, "and God will forgive
your sins."

Mark 1:4, GNT

With the Lord a day is like a
thousand years, and a thousand years
are like a day.

2 Peter 3:8, NIV

The Sovereign LORD is coming to rule with power, bringing with him the people he has rescued.

Isaiah 40:10, GNT

Surely [God] is ready to save those who honor him, and his saving presence will remain in our land.

Psalm 85:9, GNT

Put all things to the test: keep what is
good and avoid every kind of evil.

1 Thessalonians 5:21-22, GNT

As the earth bursts with spring
wildflowers, and as a garden
cascades with blossoms, so the Master,
GOD, brings righteousness into full
bloom and puts praise on display before
the nations.

Isaiah 61:11, THE MESSAGE

The light which pierces the darkness of our Advent is the first radiance of the light of Easter.

MARIA BOULDING

May God himself, the God who makes
everything holy and whole, make you
holy and whole, put you together—
spirit, soul, and body.

I Thessalonians 5:23, THE MESSAGE

Let us give glory to God! He is able to make you stand firm in your faith.

Romans 16:25, GNT

The LORD said to David, "You will always have descendants, and I will make your kingdom last forever."

2 Samuel 7:16, GNT

God sent the angel Gabriel to
Nazareth, a town in Galilee, to
a virgin . . . [whose] name was Mary.

Luke 1:26-27, NIV

The angel said, "Mary, you have nothing
to fear. God has a surprise for you: You
will become pregnant and give birth to
a son and call his name Jesus."

Luke 1:30-31, THE MESSAGE

FRIDAY · DECEMBER **16**

The angel said to Mary, "Nothing will be impossible with God."

Luke 1:37, NRSV

SATURDAY · DECEMBER **17**

To the only God, who alone is all-wise, be glory through Jesus Christ forever! Amen.

Romans 16:27, GNT

Any patch of sunlight in a wood will show you something about the sun which you could never get from reading books on astronomy. These pure and spontaneous pleasures are "patches of Godlight" in the woods of our experience.

C. S. LEWIS

FOURTH SUNDAY OF ADVENT

Mary said, "What God has done for me will never be forgotten."

Luke 1:49, THE MESSAGE

O sing unto the LORD a new song; for he hath done marvellous things.

Psalm 98:1, KJV

How wonderful it is to see a messenger coming across the mountains, bringing good news, the news of peace!

Isaiah 52:7, GNT

Long ago God spoke to our ancestors in many and various ways by the prophets, but in these last days he has spoken to us by a Son.

Hebrews 1:1-2, NRSV

[Jesus Christ] is the reflection of God's glory and the exact imprint of God's very being.

Hebrews 1:3, NRSV

[The LORD] comes to rule the earth.
He will rule the peoples of the world
with justice and fairness.

Psalm 98:9, GNT

CHRISTMAS EVE

In the beginning was the Word, and
the Word was with God, and the Word
was God.

John 1:1, NIV

Lord Jesus Christ, Thou Son of the Most High, Prince of Peace, be born again into our world. Wherever there is war in this world, wherever there is pain, wherever there is loneliness, wherever there is no hope, come, thou long-expected one, with healing in thy wings.

FREDERICK BUECHNER

CHRISTMAS DAY

The Word became flesh and blood, and
moved into the neighborhood.
We saw the glory with our own eyes,
the one-of-a-kind glory, like Father,
like Son.

John 1:14, THE MESSAGE

In union with Christ and through our faith in him we have the boldness to go into God's presence with all confidence.

Ephesians 3:12, GNT

[God] opens a place in his heart for the down-and-out, he restores the wretched of the earth.

Psalm 72:13, THE MESSAGE

Arise, shine; for your light has come,
and the glory of the LORD has risen
upon you.

Isaiah 60:1, NRSV

People who have never heard of God
and those who have heard of him all
their lives . . . stand on the same ground
before God.

Ephesians 3:6, THE MESSAGE

[God] rescues the poor who call to him,
and those who are needy and neglected.

Psalm 72:12, GNT

On coming to the house, [the
Magi] saw the child with his mother
Mary, and they bowed down and
worshiped him.

Matthew 2:11, NIV

ACKNOWLEDGMENTS

JANUARY

Roberta Porter, "Given," *Alive Now* (January–February 2005), 6. Copyright © 2004 by The Upper Room. Used by permission.

Wendy M. Wright, *The Vigil: Keeping Watch in the Season of Christ's Coming* (Nashville, TN: Upper Room Books, 1992), 158.

John O'Donohue, *Anam Cara: A Book of Celtic Wisdom* (New York: HarperCollins Publishers, 1997), 15.

Henri J. M. Nouwen, *Making All Things New: An Invitation to the Spiritual Life* (San Francisco: HarperSanFrancisco, 1981), 51.

Maxie Dunnam, *Let Me Say That Again* (Nashville, TN: Upper Room Books, 1996), unpaged.

FEBRUARY

Maria Boulding, *The Coming of God,* 3rd ed. (Conception, MO: The Printery House, 2000), 42.

Sue Monk Kidd, *When the Heart Waits: Spiritual Direction for Life's Sacred Questions* (San Francisco: Harper & Row, 1990), 4.

Joan Chittister, *Called to Question: A Spiritual Memoir* (New York: Sheed & Ward, 2004), 185.

Pamela C. Hawkins, *Simply Wait: Cultivating Stillness in the Season of Advent* (Nashville, TN: Upper Room Books, 2007), 43.

MARCH

Thomas Merton, *New Seeds of Contemplation* (New York: New Directions Books, 1961), 29.

Esther de Waal, *Lost in Wonder: Rediscovering the Spiritual Art of Attentiveness* (Collegeville, MN: Liturgical Press, 2003), 82.

Joan Chittister, *Called to Question: A Spiritual Memoir* (New York: Sheed & Ward, 2004), 44.

Mother Teresa, *Meditations from A Simple Path* (New York: Ballantine Books, 1996), 53.

APRIL

Sam Hamilton-Poore, *Earth Gospel: A Guide to Prayer for God's Creation* (Nashville, TN: Upper Room Books, 2008), 67.

Robert Lowry, "How Can I Keep from Singing?" in *The Faith We Sing* (Nashville, TN: Abingdon Press, 2000), no. 2212.

Pamela C. Hawkins, *The Awkward Season: Prayers for Lent* (Nashville: Upper Room Books, 2009), 13.

Fanny J. Crosby, "Jesus, Keep Me Near the Cross," in *The United Methodist Hymnal* (Nashville, TN: The United Methodist Publishing House, 1989), no. 301.

MAY

Macrina Wiederkehr, *Seasons of Your Heart: Prayers and Reflections, Revised and Expanded* (San Francisco: HarperSanFranciso, 1991), 5.

Susan Briehl, "Living in the Presence of God," in *On Our Way: Christian Practices for Living a Whole Life*, ed. Dorothy C. Bass and Susan R. Briehl (Nashville: Upper Room Books, 2009), 204.

Mary Lou Redding, "Prayer Workshop: Job's Self-Examination," *The Upper Room* (May–June 2009), 41.

Hildegard of Bingen, quoted in *Teachings of the Christian Mystics*, ed. Andrew Harvey (Boston: Shambhala Publications, 1998), 67.

Saint Columbanus, quoted in Esther de Waal, *Lost in Wonder: Rediscovering the Spiritual Art of Attentiveness* (Collegeville, MN: Liturgical Press, 2003), 22.

JUNE

John Cassian, *Conferences,* The Classics of Western Spirituality (Mahwah, NJ: Paulist Press, 1985), 42.

Mother Teresa, *Meditations from A Simple Path* (New York: Ballantine Books, 1996), 5.

Richard J. Foster, *Celebration of Discipline: The Path to Spiritual Growth*, 20th anniversary edition (San Francisco: HarperSanFrancisco, 1998), 93.

Lynne M. Babb, *Sabbath Keeping: Finding Freedom in the Rhythms of Rest* (Downers Grove, IL: InterVarsity Press, 2005), 96.

JULY

Johann Arndt, *True Christianity*, trans. Peter Erb (New York: Paulist Press, 1979), 163.

The Complete Thérèse of Lisieux, trans. and ed. Robert J. Edmonson (Brewster, MA: Paraclete Press, 2009), xxiv.

John O'Donohue, *Anam Cara: A Book of Celtic Wisdom* (New York: HarperCollins, 1997), 84–85.

Mary Lou Redding, *The Power of a Focused Heart: 8 Life Lessons from the Beatitudes* (Nashville: Upper Room Books, 2006), 31.

Thomas Merton, *New Seeds of Contemplation* (New York: New Directions Books, 1961), 221.

AUGUST

Mechthild of Magdeburg, quoted in *Teachings of the Christian Mystics*, ed. Andrew Harvey (Boston: Shambhala Publications, 1998), 82.

Flannery O'Connor, *The Habit of Being: The Letters of Flannery O'Connor* (New York: Farrar, Straus and Giroux, 1979), 452.

Jeremy Langford, "Where in the (Postmodern) World Is God?" in *Walking with God in a Fragile World*, ed. James Langford and Leroy S. Rouner (New York: Roman & Littlefield Publishers, 2003), 97.

Kenneth Gibble, "Understanding Forgiveness," *Alive Now* (March–April 2003), 8. Copyright © 2003 by The Upper Room. Used by permission.

SEPTEMBER
Anthony de Mello: Writings Selected with an Introduction by William Dych (Maryknoll, NY: Orbis Books, 1999), 113.

Catherine of Siena, *A Life of Total Prayer: Selected Writings of Catherine of Siena,* ed. Keith Beasley-Topliffe (Nashville, TN: Upper Room Books, 2000), 65.

Joan Chittister, *Called to Question: A Spiritual Memoir* (New York: Sheed & Ward, 2004), 178.

Oswald Chambers, *My Utmost for His Highest: An Updated Edition in Today's Language*, ed. James Reimann (Grand Rapids, MI: Discovery House Publishers, 1992), reading for October 1.

OCTOBER
Francis of Assisi, "The Song of the Sun," in *Teachings of the Christian Mystics*, ed. Andrew Harvey (Boston: Shambhala Publications, 1998), 78.

Saint Francis de Sales, quoted on Oblates of St. Francis de Sales Wilmington–Philadelphia Province Web site: www.oblates.org/spirituality/sundays_salesian/2006_4_30.php

David Steindl-Rast, *Gratefulness, the Heart of Prayer: An Approach to Life in Fullness* (New York: Paulist Press, 1984), 17.

Teresa of Avila, *Interior Castle* (Notre Dame, IN: Ave Maria Press, 2007), 157.

Macrina Wiederkehr, *Seasons of Your Heart: Prayers and Reflections, Revised and Expanded* (San Francisco: HarperSanFrancisco, 1991), 7.

NOVEMBER
Dom Helder Câmara, in *The Westminster Collection of Christian Quotations*, comp. Martin H. Manser (Louisville, KY: Westminster John Knox Press, 2001), 181.

John Kirvan, *God Hunger: Discovering the Mystic in All of Us* (Notre Dame, IN: Sorin Books, 1999), 62.

Meister Eckhart, in *This Sacred Earth: Religion, Nature, Environment,* ed. Roger Gottlieb (New York: Routledge, 1996), 46.

Evelyn Underhill, *Light of Christ* (Harrisburg, PA: Morehouse Publishing, 1982).

DECEMBER

Beth A. Richardson, *The Uncluttered Heart: Making Room for God During Advent and Christmas* (Nashville: Upper Room Books, 2009), 12.

Maria Boulding, *The Coming of God*, 3rd ed. (Conception, MO: The Printery House, 2000), 190.

C. S. Lewis, *Letters to Malcolm: Chiefly on Prayer* (New York: Harvest Books/Harcourt, 2002), 91.

Frederick Buechner, *The Hungering Dark* (New York: Seabury Press, 1969), 16.